AF687997

Chatbots & AI Support Agents

Build Smart Assistants With ChatGPT, Tiledesk & Intercom

By Joe Correa

Published by Live Stronger Faster

Copyright © 2025 by Joe Correa

All rights reserved.

No part of this publication may be reproduced, distributed, or transmitted in any form or by any means—electronic, mechanical, photocopying, recording, or otherwise—without the prior written permission of the publisher, except in the case of brief quotations embodied in critical reviews and certain other noncommercial uses permitted by copyright law.

This book is for educational and informational purposes only. The author and publisher are not engaged in rendering legal, financial, or other professional advice. Readers should consult a qualified professional before making any financial decisions.

First Edition

Table of Contents

Introduction 5

Chapter 1: The Foundation of AI Support (Understanding How Modern Chatbots Work) 10

Chapter 2: Designing a Support Bot That Feels Human, Reliable, and Intelligent 17

Chapter 3: Mastering Intent Recognition (Teaching Your AI to Understand What Customers Really Mean) 24

Chapter 4: Building Perfect Conversation Flows (How to Guide Users to Fast and Accurate Solutions) 31

Chapter 5: Knowledge Bases & Training Data (Teaching Your AI Support Agent What It Needs to Know) 38

Chapter 6: Handling Emotions, Frustration, and High-Stress Conversations With AI 45

Chapter 7: Building Dynamic FAQs, Troubleshooting Trees & Decision Paths 52

Chapter 8: Integrations & Automations (Connecting Your AI Agent to CRMs, Ticketing Systems & Real Workflows) 59

Chapter 9: Escalation Logic (Teaching Your AI When & How to Pass Conversations to Humans) 66

Chapter 10: Analytics, Feedback Loops & Continuous Improvement for AI Support Systems 73

Chapter 11 Twenty Practical Prompts to Build, Train & Improve Your AI Support Agent 80

Where to Insert the Prompts 85

Epilogue 88

Introduction

Customer support has quietly become the new competitive battlefield. Every company, no matter the size, now competes with global brands that offer instant replies, 24/7 support availability, personalized recommendations, and lightning-fast issue resolution. People expect help right now—not in a few hours, and definitely not tomorrow. They want answers immediately, they want accuracy, and they want the experience to feel human. But most businesses can't keep up with that expectation. The cost of maintaining a full support team is high. The stress of constant inquiries is exhausting. And the moment a company falls behind, customers leave for competitors who respond faster. That's where chatbots and AI support agents begin to transform everything.

This book is designed to give you the ability to build those agents yourself—without writing code, without hiring developers, and without needing years of tech training. The world has shifted, and businesses now rely on ChatGPT-powered chatbots, Tiledesk conversational flows, Intercom AI assistants, and hybrid support systems that combine automated reasoning with human fallback. What used to take an entire department can now be built by one person using no-code tools, automation platforms, and well-designed AI prompts. If you've ever wanted to build a smart support agent that can answer questions, guide customers through complicated processes, reduce workload, and increase conversions, you're in the right place.

Chatbots today are not the cold, robotic systems of the past. Modern AI support agents understand context, maintain conversation history, identify user intent, and adjust tone dynamically. They can troubleshoot issues, collect data, escalate tickets to human agents, and even recover abandoned leads. And because these agents run on top of powerful large-language-models, they learn and adapt based on examples you feed them. For the first time in history, anyone can build a customer-service system that feels intelligent, responsive, and deeply personal—no programming degree required.

Businesses everywhere are shifting to AI-powered support because customers prefer immediate help over waiting in line or navigating phone menus. A well-trained chatbot can reduce support tickets by 50–80% while improving customer satisfaction. It can greet visitors, ask questions, suggest solutions, provide tutorials, collect forms, qualify leads, and route complex issues directly to the appropriate human worker. This combination of automation and personalization allows you to scale a support system that grows with your business instead of slowing it down. The tools you'll learn in this book—ChatGPT, Tiledesk, Intercom, Make.com, Zapier, Google Sheets, and advanced AI prompt structures—will give you the ability to build support bots that are both powerful and flexible. You'll learn how to design conversational logic, structure knowledge bases, build decision trees, handle objections, gather data, authenticate user identity, and escalate conversations in a smooth, natural flow. More importantly, you'll learn how to make your chatbot feel like a high-level expert—one that customers trust, enjoy interacting with, and rely on for consistent help.

This book is structured to guide you through every layer of building a no-code AI support agent, from simple FAQ bots to advanced multi-channel support systems that integrate email, website chat, WhatsApp, SMS, and social platforms. You'll discover how to teach your agent the voice of your brand so it replies professionally. You'll learn how to analyze user intent and build logic that makes conversations more accurate. And you'll understand how to avoid the biggest mistakes companies make when launching chatbots, including over-automating, under-training, and failing to provide clear fallback paths.

Even if you've never built a chatbot before, this book will show you step-by-step how to construct systems that handle support tasks with clarity and precision. You'll learn how to use AI to write replies, summarize tickets, draft support instructions, and generate onboarding sequences. And you'll discover how to deploy agents on your website, inside apps, through CRMs, and across your communication channels. From the moment a customer arrives to the moment they solve their problem, your AI agent will be ready to guide them with speed and intelligence.

More importantly, this book will give you the confidence to build solutions that save time and money. Customer support is expensive. Hiring is expensive. Training teams is expensive. But building an AI system that performs thousands of actions in minutes is now accessible to anyone with imagination and the willingness to learn. You'll gain the skills to create support flows that are reliable, scalable, and deeply human-friendly—without ever writing a line of code.

This book is part of a larger series designed to help you build AI agents across multiple categories: voice, business automation, research, data analysis, ecommerce, monetization, and workflow design. But this volume is one of the most essential, because customer interaction is the heartbeat of every business. Support agents are the direct connection between a company and its customers. When they operate at a high level, retention rises. Sales increase.

Complaints go down. Experiences improve. And your brand becomes known for reliability and responsiveness.

By the end of this book, you will not only know how to build a chatbot—you will know how to build a support agent that feels alive. You'll understand how to design interactions that feel natural and helpful. You'll know how to automate tasks that used to take hours. And you'll be ready to build a future-proof support system that grows with your business, supports customers around the world, and works tirelessly without breaks, salaries, or burnout.

Welcome to Book 6 of the No-Code AI Agent Builder Series. Welcome to the future of intelligent customer support. Welcome to the era where you become the architect of AI experiences that change how people are helped, served, and supported.

Chapter 1

The Foundation of AI Support (Understanding How Modern Chatbots Work)

Customer support has evolved dramatically in the last decade. Traditional support systems relied on human agents handling every inquiry manually, leading to long wait times, inconsistent answers, and high operational costs. Today, businesses are shifting to AI-driven support systems that offer instant responses, availability around the clock, and consistent accuracy. Modern chatbots are no longer simple scripted tools; they are intelligent conversational agents powered by large-language models, intent classification, memory, and context awareness. Understanding how these systems truly work is the foundation upon which every powerful support bot is built. Before you design conversational flows or connect automation tools, you must understand the mechanics behind AI-driven support assistants.

At the core of every modern AI chatbot lies a language model—such as GPT-4 or a specialized model integrated into platforms like Tiledesk or Intercom. These models do not rely on predefined scripts alone. Instead, they analyze user input, identify intent, interpret context, and generate natural language responses instantly. They can handle clarifying questions, maintain multi-step conversations, and provide information based on instructions, knowledge bases, or previous examples you give them. This means that the quality of your chatbot depends largely on the quality of the instructions, training data, and conversational structure you design. Unlike old chatbots that answered only specific keywords, modern AI agents interpret full sentences and use reasoning to determine the best answer.

The next element is intent recognition. When a customer asks a question, the chatbot must identify what they want. Is the user asking for a refund? Troubleshooting a product? Requesting onboarding help? Seeking a password reset? Intent recognition helps the bot understand the underlying purpose behind a user's message. You will learn how to build intent lists, define example queries, train your bot on different scenarios, and create fallback rules. This is crucial because a chatbot that misinterprets intent will lead to frustration. When done correctly, intent recognition becomes the backbone of a highly effective support agent that interacts smoothly and accurately every time.

A powerful AI support system also relies on structured knowledge. This can include FAQs, documentation, policy pages, tutorials, troubleshooting guides, and curated instructions you provide. Instead of forcing users to read long pages, your chatbot can reference these materials to produce clear, concise answers. Later in this book, you will build your own centralized knowledge base that your chatbot uses to produce fast, authoritative responses. A well-built knowledge base allows your bot to give consistent answers that reflect your brand's official policies, tone, and accuracy. Without this, chatbots become unclear, inconsistent, or overly generic.

The fourth foundational component is conversation design. This includes the architecture of your chatbot's message flows, escalation paths, fallback behaviors, tone, and persona. You will learn how to design conversations that feel fluid and natural. Support bots must not only answer questions—they must guide users, ask clarifying questions, and provide structured steps. You'll explore techniques like branching logic, dynamic answers, emotion-aware responses, and guided troubleshooting. Conversation design is what makes a bot feel personal, human-like, and trustworthy. When done correctly, it turns a simple chatbot into a reliable assistant that enhances the customer experience.

Finally, automation and integration transform your chatbot from a simple answering system into a powerful operational tool. With Make.com, Zapier, and built-in CRM connections, your bot can create tickets, send emails, assign tasks to teams, update databases, authenticate customers, and escalate complex issues. You'll learn how to integrate your chatbot into your support ecosystem so it becomes a seamless part of your workflow. This allows you to scale support operations without hiring large teams, freeing your time and increasing customer satisfaction. In this chapter, you've learned the foundational concepts that will guide the rest of this book: how modern chatbots work, what powers them, and why they are essential in today's business landscape.

"The Night the Support Center Changed Forever"

When the final email of the day arrived, Mia Alvarez felt her shoulders sink with exhaustion. She ran customer support for a growing software company, and her small team had already handled more than two hundred messages. The clock showed 8:17 p.m., long after business hours, yet the inbox kept filling. Refund requests. Password resets. Troubleshooting questions. Endless variations of the same issues. She looked across the empty office, remembering how the CEO had told her, "We'll automate soon." But automation never came—only more customers, more questions, and more pressure. She sat back, rubbing her temples, wondering how she could keep this pace without burning out her team.

Then something unusual happened. A notification flashed on her screen: "New message – answered." But no one was logged in. Confused, Mia clicked open the message thread. A customer had asked about a login issue, and the reply had already been sent—politely, accurately, and instantly. Her heart raced for a moment. Was it a glitch? A hack? She scrolled up. More messages had been answered automatically: a refund policy explanation, a tutorial link, a troubleshooting guide. Each reply matched the company's tone perfectly. Then a note appeared from the CEO: "Mia, check your dashboard. It's finally live."

She opened the internal dashboard and saw a new module blinking: "AI Support Agent – Activated." A mix of relief and disbelief washed over her. The agent had been trained on their FAQs, policies, and workflows. It knew how to handle basic issues, ask follow-up questions, escalate when needed, and keep tone consistent. As she watched, the bot handled three more inquiries—smoothly, intelligently, without hesitation. But the moment that changed everything came when a frustrated customer wrote a long message complaining about an error they couldn't fix. Mia braced herself, expecting the bot to stumble. Instead, it asked a clarifying question, interpreted the customer's tone, offered step-by-step guidance, and even created a support ticket automatically. The customer replied moments later: "Thank you so much. This was faster than any support I've ever used." Mia stared at the screen in silence. For the first time in months, the overwhelming feeling of drowning under an endless support backlog lifted from her chest. The AI agent didn't replace her team—it empowered them. It handled repetitive tasks instantly, giving her team space to breathe and focus on high-value conversations. She felt that shift deep in her core: this was not the future arriving someday—this was the present transforming right before her eyes. The more she watched the agent work, the more she realized something profound: customer support wasn't just being automated; it was being reimagined.

Over the next few days, Mia studied how the AI handled conversations. It asked the right questions, knew when to escalate, and never lost patience. It guided customers through complex steps with clarity she wished she'd had months earlier. She discovered how the system worked—intent recognition, knowledge bases, integration with their database, escalation triggers, and automated workflows. Each piece came together like a symphony of intelligence and efficiency. Mia had spent years thinking support required endless manual labor. Now she saw how powerful an AI support agent could be when designed with care, powered by the right instructions, and integrated into the heart of the business.

One night, she stayed late at the office again, but this time it wasn't from stress. She watched the AI handle conversations in real time, answering messages with a balance of precision and empathy. She smiled, realizing this was the turning point she had been waiting for. The fatigue that once clouded her days was replaced with excitement. She imagined scaling globally, offering 24/7 support, and building a customer experience that felt personal and immediate. For the first time, she wasn't just reacting—she was leading the future of her department.

When the CEO walked into the office the next morning, Mia greeted him with a confidence he hadn't seen before. "It's working," she said. "And this... this is just the beginning." Together they looked at the dashboard, watching the AI agent carry the weight that once overwhelmed them. Mia realized that she wasn't just witnessing a technological upgrade—she was witnessing a transformation that would change customer support forever. And she knew she was ready for the next step: learning how to build and refine these AI support agents herself, shaping a system that could grow with the company and redefine what customer support truly meant.

Chapter 2

Designing a Support Bot That Feels Human, Reliable, and Intelligent

Before building flows or connecting platforms like Tiledesk, Intercom, or ChatGPT, you must first understand how to design a support bot that feels genuinely helpful. Many businesses make the mistake of jumping directly into tool setup without laying the foundations for a human-like conversation experience. A chatbot is not simply a machine that answers questions; it is the first line of communication, the emotional filter, and the tone-setter for your brand. Customer trust begins with the way your support agent communicates. If your chatbot feels robotic, dismissive, unhelpful, or too generic, customers disengage instantly. That is why designing your bot's personality, tone, behavior, and conversation strategy is the most important step in building a world-class AI support system.

The first element of human-like design is persona. Your chatbot needs identity, voice, tone, and a consistent communication style. This doesn't mean adding humor or overly casual traits—it means creating a personality that reflects your business values. Support bots should be empathetic, clear, patient, and structured. A well-designed persona reduces misunderstandings, improves clarity, and keeps the entire support experience aligned with your brand. Later in this book, you will craft your agent's persona profile, including tone rules, escalation language, greeting style, and fallback behavior. When a bot's persona is clear, customers feel like they're talking to a knowledgeable, calm, and capable representative.

Next, your support bot must understand context. Context includes the history of the conversation, the user's previous questions, the product or service being discussed, and the emotional tone of the user. Modern AI allows your bot to remember details within a session, track user needs across multiple steps, and adjust its communication based on sentiment. Without context, users feel like they're repeating themselves. With context, the conversation becomes seamless, effortless, and efficient. You will learn how to use memory prompts, structured fields, and conditional logic so your chatbot always knows what's going on in the conversation.

The third element of human-like design is clarity. Support agents must simplify information, break down complicated steps, and present answers in a structured format. Clarity is achieved by using short sentences, numbered steps, bulleted troubleshooting instructions, and precisely-worded confirmations. AI chatbots excel in clarity when given well-written training prompts and templates. This means giving your bot structured examples of how to respond: how to troubleshoot, ask questions, provide instructions, collect information, and offer solutions. You are not teaching the AI to sound human—you are teaching it how to communicate effectively.

A fourth element is emotional intelligence. AI cannot feel emotions, but it can mimic emotional awareness with the right instructions. If a customer is confused, frustrated, or worried, an emotionally aware agent acknowledges their feelings before providing a solution. This makes customers feel heard rather than dismissed. You will learn how to incorporate sentiment detection, empathetic phrasing templates, and dynamic tone adjustments into your bot's design. This is the difference between an agent that simply "responds" and one that truly "supports."

A fifth element is controlled conversation flow. A well-designed AI support agent never overwhelms the user with excessive information. It asks the right questions, in the right order, and only when needed. This requires guiding the conversation with subtle prompts and decision points. You will learn how to structure flows that move users forward naturally—from problem identification to resolution. This includes clarifying questions, fallback questions, and escalation triggers. The best bots do not depend on long user messages; they lead the user step by step.

Finally, human-like design depends on consistency. Every answer your bot gives must match brand policies, product knowledge, and official guidelines. A support bot must never guess. It must never invent. It must never contradict documentation. To achieve this, you will learn how to build a knowledge system that the bot pulls from and how to set strict guardrails through system prompts. The goal is not only to automate conversations but to automate them with accuracy, reliability, and professionalism.

When these elements come together—persona, context, clarity, emotional intelligence, structured flow, and consistency—you build a support agent that feels like a calm, friendly, helpful expert working for your company. Customers respect it. Teams rely on it. Businesses scale with it. And you become the architect who brought all these pieces together. This chapter sets the stage for designing a world-class AI support agent that elevates customer experience far beyond simple automation.

"The Conversation That Should've Gone Wrong"

When the message came in, Leo Soriano knew it was the type of inquiry that could go sideways fast. The customer had just purchased their premium software upgrade and couldn't get the new features to activate. The message read like a storm of frustration—long paragraphs, capital letters, and the unmistakable tone of someone ready to demand a refund. In the past, Leo's support team dreaded messages like these. They never went smoothly. But today was different. Today the company's new AI support agent was running live for its second week.

Leo watched as the customer typed three more messages in rapid succession. Complaints, confusion, threats to cancel. The kind of emotional intensity that usually needed a senior support member to calm things down. Leo hovered his cursor over the conversation, ready to jump in manually. But before he could type, the AI agent responded. It did not offer a generic apology. It did not try to over-explain. It opened with something disarming, something Leo had never seen a machine write so naturally: "I'm really sorry this is causing so much stress. Let me help you fix it right away." Seven simple words—empathetic, confident, and human.

The customer paused. The typing indicator disappeared. Then reappeared slowly. "Okay... thank you." It was subtle, but Leo noticed the shift. The intensity softened. The AI agent continued gently, asking one clarifying question. No long paragraphs. No overwhelming instructions. Just one simple question that narrowed the issue instantly. When the customer responded, the bot recognized the exact problem: an outdated browser extension blocking the activation script. The AI delivered instructions in short, precise steps. The customer followed them. Within minutes, the issue was resolved.

Then came the message no one expected: "Wow... this was the best support I've ever had." Leo leaned back in his chair, stunned. The person who had threatened to cancel minutes earlier was now thanking the support team. But the AI agent wasn't finished. It asked if the customer wanted a walkthrough video for their next steps. The customer agreed. The bot automatically sent a link, logged the issue in the CRM, and marked the conversation as "resolved with satisfaction." Leo felt something shift inside him. This wasn't just automation—it was transformation.

Later that evening, Leo replayed the conversation to understand how the AI pulled it off. He saw the agent recognize sentiment, adjust its tone, simplify instructions, and maintain calm from beginning to end. It never rushed. Never over-explained. Never broke character. It behaved like the best version of a human agent—one who never got tired, frustrated, or overwhelmed. Leo realized in that moment that the AI wasn't replacing his team; it was elevating them. Instead of drowning in emotional conversations, his agents could now focus on building relationships, handling advanced issues, and improving processes. Two days later, the CEO called Leo into the office. "Congratulations," she told him. "Our customer satisfaction score just hit the highest level in company history." Leo smiled, thinking back to the conversation that should've gone wrong—the one that changed everything. The AI agent didn't just solve a technical issue; it healed a customer's frustration, restored trust, and protected the brand. It had shown Leo a new truth: the future of support wasn't cold or robotic. It was warm, human-like, and deeply intelligent.

As he left the office that day, Leo felt proud—not just of the technology, but of what it meant for the future of their company. They weren't just building software. They were building experiences. They were building trust. And now, with AI by their side, they had the tools to support every customer the way they always wished they could.

Chapter 3

Mastering Intent Recognition (Teaching Your AI to Understand What Customers Really Mean)

One of the most important skills your AI support agent must have is the ability to understand intent. Intent is the underlying purpose behind a customer's message—the real problem they are trying to solve. A customer may write a full paragraph, a single sentence, or just a frustrated "It doesn't work!" and your chatbot must identify what they actually need. Intent recognition is the foundation that determines whether your AI agent will feel intelligent or clueless. When intent is correctly identified, the conversation flows smoothly, resolutions are fast, and customers feel supported. When intent is misunderstood, frustration rises, and automation breaks down. Mastering intent recognition is therefore essential for designing a reliable support agent.

To understand intent, your chatbot must use both AI reasoning and structured training data. Large-language models naturally understand patterns in human language, but they become dramatically more accurate when given explicit intent categories and examples. You will learn how to create a master list of customer intents—refund requests, password resets, onboarding help, troubleshooting, feature explanations, billing issues, upgrade questions, cancellation concerns, and more. Each intent category must include example phrases, variations, synonyms, and emotional versions. This allows your AI to map user messages to the correct intent regardless of how they're phrased.

Once you build intent categories, you must create clear rules about how the bot should respond to each one. Some intents require immediate action, such as "I want a refund" or "I can't log in." Others require follow-up questions to gather details, such as "My screen is frozen" or "Your tool isn't working." Your chatbot must learn when to ask clarifying questions, when to provide direct solutions, and when to escalate. Intent recognition is not only about identifying what the user wants—it's about designing the correct path that follows. Later in this book, you will create intent-response matrices that map every intent to its ideal conversational flow.

Another essential element is multi-intent handling. Customers often mix several intentions in one message. For example: "I bought the upgrade, but the features don't work, and now I'm thinking about canceling." This includes onboarding, troubleshooting, and potential cancellation—all in one sentence. A poorly designed chatbot will choose only one intent and ignore the rest. A properly trained AI agent recognizes multiple intents and responds in structured order, addressing each one clearly and professionally. This skill alone can reduce misunderstandings, prevent customer frustration, and dramatically improve satisfaction.

Emotion plays a role in intent recognition as well. Customers sometimes use emotional language instead of describing the actual problem. Statements like “I am so frustrated right now” or “This is ridiculous” reveal emotional intent, not technical intent. A well-designed bot acknowledges emotions before addressing the issue. Emotional intent is often the key to restoring trust, and your bot must learn how to navigate it. You will build templates that help your AI handle emotional tone gracefully while still gathering necessary information.

The final step in mastering intent recognition is continuous improvement. Even the best AI needs refinement as customer behaviors evolve. You will learn how to review transcripts, analyze misunderstood intents, and update categories and examples. This iterative process allows your chatbot to become smarter over time, reducing errors and increasing accuracy. Continuous training ensures that your AI stays aligned with your brand, products, and support workflows. Intent recognition is not a one-time setup—it is an ongoing discipline that keeps your bot operating at the highest level. When you combine well-structured intent categories, dynamic flow rules, emotional recognition, multi-intent handling, and continuous refinement, you create an AI support agent that understands customers deeply and consistently. Intent recognition is the secret behind support interactions that feel smooth, intelligent, and effortless. By mastering this skill, you will build support bots that customers trust—and that your team relies on every day.

"The Question Behind the Question"

When Maya Patel started her shift at the customer support center, she expected the usual stream of questions. Most users needed help logging in or resetting passwords. But one message stood out immediately. It came from a long-time customer named Jordan, who wrote: "I've been using your app for years, but I'm seriously thinking about switching to a competitor. Everything feels off lately. Can someone explain why this update broke everything?" The message radiated frustration, disappointment, and urgency. Maya knew conversations like this required careful handling. Normally, she would step in personally. But today, she watched as the AI support agent took the lead.

The AI agent didn't respond defensively or with technical jargon. It paused for a moment, then replied with a gentle, empathetic tone that surprised Maya: "I'm really sorry you're running into trouble. I want to understand exactly what changed on your end so I can help you quickly. Can you tell me which feature isn't working the way you expect?" It didn't try to solve anything prematurely. It didn't challenge the customer's frustration. It simply acknowledged the emotion and asked one simple clarifying question. Jordan immediately replied with a calmer message describing issues with syncing, notifications, and account switching.

Maya watched as the AI recognized multiple intentions: troubleshooting, dissatisfaction, confusion about the update, and potential cancellation. Instead of focusing on only one, the agent addressed each piece in an organized, human-like flow. "Thanks for sharing that. I can help with all of these. Let's start with the sync issue—it's usually quick to fix. After that, I'll walk you through notifications and show you what changed in the update." Jordan agreed, and for the first time in the conversation, the tone shifted from anger to cooperation. The AI guided him through a few steps, each short and clear. Within minutes, the sync issue was resolved.

Then something unexpected happened. As the AI moved to the notification settings, it detected a deeper intention—fear of losing data. Jordan briefly mentioned backing up photos, but the AI caught the emotional nuance. "Just to reassure you," it added gently, "none of your data was lost during the update. Everything is fully backed up and safe." Jordan replied instantly: "Oh thank God. That was my biggest worry." That single acknowledgment changed the entire conversation. Maya realized the AI hadn't just solved a technical problem—it had identified the real underlying concern.

The agent continued with steady confidence, walking Jordan through the new interface and explaining features he had overlooked. By the end of the conversation, he wrote: "Thank you. I'm staying with your app. This actually helped a lot more than I expected." Maya couldn't believe how the AI had not only salvaged the customer relationship but strengthened it. After the conversation ended, she reviewed the transcript. The AI had identified four different intents—technical, emotional, informational, and retention-related—and handled each one with precision.

Hours later, when Maya met with her team, she shared what she had seen. "It's not just answering questions," she told them. "It's understanding what the customer actually means—even when they don't say it directly." The others nodded, realizing the importance of intent in every interaction. The AI wasn't replacing them; it was giving them a level of clarity they had never had before. They could now focus on complex cases while the AI handled the subtle emotional and technical layers hidden inside daily messages. That night, as Maya prepared to leave the office, she remembered something one of her old mentors had told her: “In customer support, the real question is almost never the first thing they ask.” She smiled, now understanding exactly how powerful it was to have an AI assistant that could uncover the true question behind the question. And she knew this was only the beginning of what intent recognition could do for the future of their support team.

Chapter 4

Building Perfect Conversation Flows (How to Guide Users to Fast and Accurate Solutions)

Conversation flow is the backbone of every successful AI support agent. No matter how advanced your language model is, or how well your intents are structured, your bot will struggle if the flow of the conversation is unclear, chaotic, or poorly organized. A support bot must guide users through a predictable, reliable process that delivers answers quickly while maintaining clarity and professionalism. This chapter will teach you how to design clean, logical, human-friendly flows that ensure your AI agent always leads customers toward resolution instead of confusion.

The first rule of conversation flow design is simplicity. Most users don't want long paragraphs or complex instructions. They want short, clear steps that feel easy to follow. Your bot must break down complex issues into smaller questions: "Is the issue happening on mobile or desktop?" "Did you receive an error message?" "Can you confirm if you're logged in?" These clarifying questions accomplish two things: they reduce the user's cognitive load and help the bot pinpoint the problem accurately. When you design flows with simplicity in mind, your AI avoids overwhelming users and ensures each step feels manageable.

The second rule is sequence control. Every support task must follow a logical order, and your chatbot must guide users through that order naturally. This means structuring your flows around decision trees, conditional branches, and sequential troubleshooting steps. A well-designed conversation flow moves like a guided path: identify the issue, gather context, deliver the solution, verify success, and close with a helpful follow-up. When flows follow predictable patterns, your AI agent stays consistent and customers feel supported from start to finish.

The third rule is dynamic adaptation. A modern AI support agent must be flexible and adjust to user input in real time. If a user jumps ahead, skips steps, or provides additional details out of order, your bot must adapt without breaking the conversation. This requires building prompts that allow for branching responses. You'll learn how to design adaptive flows that read the user's intention and continue the conversation smoothly. Adaptation is what makes a support bot feel intelligent instead of rigid.

The fourth rule is escalation awareness. A strong support agent knows its limits. When an issue is too complex, sensitive, or requires human verification, your bot must escalate gracefully. This means explaining why escalation is needed, gathering necessary details, and transferring the conversation smoothly to a human agent. Escalation is not a failure—it is a sign of responsible design. When a bot escalates at the right time, customers appreciate that they are being handled with care instead of being forced through automation that cannot help them.

The fifth rule is tone consistency across the flow. Each step in the conversation must maintain the bot's persona—calm, professional, friendly, and clear. Tone consistency prevents confusion and builds trust. You will learn how to write reusable templates for confirmations, instructions, questions, and emotional acknowledgments so your bot never sounds inconsistent or robotic. Consistent tone reinforces brand voice and makes interactions feel familiar, predictable, and comforting.

The sixth rule is resolution reinforcement. At the end of every conversation, your support agent must confirm that the issue is resolved and offer additional help. Closing messages like "I'm glad we fixed that—would you like help with anything else?" or "I've documented this update in your account for future reference" create a sense of completion and professionalism. This reduces follow-up inquiries and increases customer satisfaction significantly. Great support doesn't end when the solution is delivered; it ends when the customer feels confident and taken care of.

When you design conversation flows using these principles—simplicity, sequence control, dynamic adaptation, escalation awareness, tone consistency, and resolution reinforcement—you create a support agent that feels natural, reliable, and human-aligned. Customers feel guided rather than pushed, supported rather than overwhelmed. This chapter prepares you to build the structured frameworks that will power your AI agent throughout the rest of the book.

"The Map That Couldn't Be Broken"

On a rainy Wednesday morning, the support center felt unusually tense. The company had just launched a massive update to their platform, and the team braced themselves for a surge of confused customers. They had spent weeks preparing documentation, training videos, and webinars, but they all knew that once users got their hands on the new interface, unexpected issues would appear. At the center of the room, Ava Flores, the head of support engineering, watched the team nervously. But she wasn't worried—not this time. Their new AI support agent had been redesigned with a completely new conversation flow, built carefully, piece by piece, like a map that could not be broken.

At exactly 9:04 a.m., the first message came in. A user named Ethan wrote: "Everything looks different. I can't find anything anymore." In the past, this kind of message led to long back-and-forth exchanges that drained the team's energy. But Ava watched with curiosity as the AI agent responded. "I know updates can feel overwhelming. I'm here to guide you. First, which part of the platform are you trying to access—projects, analytics, or account settings?" It didn't try to explain everything at once. It simply asked the first question on the map.

Ethan replied: "Analytics." The bot continued: "Great. Are you using the mobile app or the desktop version?" Ethan answered quickly: "Desktop." The AI then sent a short message with a single screenshot and one line of text: "Here's where the analytics tab moved in the new update." Ethan paused, then typed: "Oh! Found it. Thank you." Ava smiled. The flow was working exactly as designed. Step by step. Question by question. Never too much information, never too little.

But the real test came twenty minutes later when a user named Harper wrote a long, emotional message about losing access to project data. The message was frantic—multiple issues mixed together, frustration leaking through every word. Ava leaned in, knowing that chaotic conversations were historically the ones that broke bots. But the AI handled it with precision. It began with empathy, then triggered a special flow for multi-intent messages. “I hear how stressful this feels. I can help you with all of this. Let’s start with the data access issue, since that sounds most urgent.” The bot guided Harper through verification steps, checking if the project was archived, whether permissions changed, and whether the account had synced properly.

Each step felt like walking down a clear path, even though Harper’s initial message had been a storm of confusion. The AI didn’t get overwhelmed. It didn’t lose track. It didn’t jump ahead. It followed the map exactly, softly guiding Harper toward clarity. When the issue turned out to be a permission setting accidentally changed during the update, Harper typed: “I can’t believe that was it. Thank you for helping me stay calm. You handled that so clearly.”

Ava stepped back in awe. For years she had seen support agents struggle with conversations that spiraled out of control. Customers jumped between issues, changed topics, ignored steps, and typed in emotional waves that made troubleshooting nearly impossible. But today, the AI held the conversation together with an invisible structure. It adapted when Harper skipped steps. It waited patiently when she hesitated. It never lost its way. The map held firm. Later that afternoon, Ava reviewed several dozens of transcripts. Each one showed the same pattern—the AI agent guiding users through carefully designed flows that created calm, clarity, and efficiency. Even when customers introduced unexpected details, the bot adapted without losing direction. It was like watching a river flow smoothly no matter where rocks appeared. The team knew that something had changed forever.

Ava closed her laptop and gazed out the window at the fading rain. She realized that they had not simply built a chatbot—they had built an experience. A navigation system for human frustration. A guide that could turn chaos into order. And for the first time, the support team felt confident about scaling their operations without fear. The map was solid. The flows were unbreakable. And the future of their support system had never looked clearer.

Chapter 5

Knowledge Bases & Training Data (Teaching Your AI Support Agent What It Needs to Know)

A support agent is only as intelligent as the information it understands. Even the most advanced AI model will produce generic or inaccurate answers if it isn't trained with the exact knowledge your business relies on. That's why building a complete, structured knowledge base is one of the most important steps in developing your chatbot. A knowledge base acts as your bot's brain—guiding its responses, ensuring accuracy, and maintaining consistency across all customer interactions. Without it, your chatbot becomes guesswork. With it, your support agent becomes a reliable expert who always gives customers the right information.

The first step in building a powerful knowledge base is content gathering. You must collect everything your business uses to support customers: FAQs, documentation, onboarding guides, troubleshooting steps, policies, video transcripts, feature explanations, and templates. The goal is to gather raw material, not perfection. Many companies underestimate how much knowledge they already have scattered across emails, support logs, internal docs, and Slack messages. These become the foundation of your AI training data. Later, you will refine them into structured, searchable, easy-to-understand content.

Next, organization. A successful AI knowledge base is structured into categories, subcategories, and reference blocks. Instead of one giant document, you'll break everything into smaller units that your AI can reference cleanly. Examples include: "Refund Policy," "Password Reset Steps," "Troubleshooting Login Issues," "Billing Explainer," "Feature Tutorials," "Onboarding Sequence," and "Account Permissions Guide." Each piece must be written simply, clearly, and without unnecessary details. The clearer the structure, the more accurate your chatbot becomes.

The third step is standardization. Every piece of information must follow the same formatting rules. If your refund policy is written differently from your troubleshooting steps, your bot will sound inconsistent. Standardization also includes tone, terminology, and step formatting. For example, all troubleshooting instructions should follow the same structure: acknowledge, clarify, guide, confirm. All product explanations should follow the same sequence: purpose, how it works, common use cases, limitations. When content is standardized, your AI agent becomes predictable and trusted by your customers. After standardization comes training integration. This is where you connect your knowledge base to the AI environment. Some platforms allow direct ingestion, while others use embeddings, URLs, or vector databases to store information. Regardless of the method, the goal is for the AI to retrieve exactly the right information when needed. You will learn how to set system prompts, retrieval instructions, and fallback rules that prevent hallucinations. Your bot must be trained to never guess, never invent information, and always refer back to your official knowledge base.

The fifth step in developing a strong knowledge system is continuous updating. Your business will change over time—new features launch, old features are retired, pricing evolves, policies update, user needs shift. Your knowledge base must evolve with these changes. You will learn how to schedule monthly reviews, automate updates from your internal documents, and refine your training data based on real customer interactions. This ensures your AI always stays aligned with the latest version of your business.

Finally, you must teach your AI how to apply knowledge conversationally. Knowledge alone is not enough; your agent must use it effectively. This includes teaching the AI how to shorten explanations, break down steps, ask follow-up questions, and use knowledge in a human-like way. You will build conversational templates that show the bot when to reference documents, how to present instructions, and how to phrase policy explanations without sounding robotic. When you combine knowledge and communication design, your support agent becomes a true expert—accurate, confident, and helpful in every interaction.

A well-constructed knowledge base is the difference between a bot that "tries its best" and a bot that performs flawlessly. With strong training data, your AI agent becomes a trusted extension of your business—a reliable source of truth customers depend on. This chapter gives you the foundation to build that brain, ensuring your chatbot has everything it needs to support users intelligently and consistently.

"The Library That Saved the Launch"

On the morning of the company's biggest product launch, the support center felt electrified. Employees rushed between desks, marketing teams prepared the announcement emails, and engineers triple-checked the servers. The entire atmosphere buzzed with excitement and tension. At the center of the room stood Riley Chen, the lead knowledge architect, who felt the pressure more than anyone. Their last product launch had been chaotic—customers flooded the support lines with questions, and the team struggled to find answers buried in old documents. But this time was different. This time, they had a new library. Riley spent the last month building a complete knowledge base for the company's AI support agent.

Every policy, every step-by-step guide, every feature explanation, every workaround—it all lived in one place, cleanly structured, checked for accuracy, and written in a consistent tone. It was the most organized document the company had ever created. But the real test would come today. Riley's heart pounded as the launch countdown hit zero and thousands of users began logging into the platform.

Within minutes, support messages poured in. "Where's the new analytics tool?" "How do I import old files?" "Why does the dashboard look different?" Normally, this would trigger panic. But the AI agent handled each question gracefully. When a user asked how to transfer projects, the bot pulled the exact steps from the new library: clear, concise, and easy to follow. When another user asked about pricing changes, the bot used the official pricing block—perfectly worded and up-to-date. Riley watched in awe as the AI effortlessly retrieved information from the knowledge base, weaving it into friendly, human-like replies.

Then came the real challenge. A long message appeared from a major enterprise customer, filled with urgent questions about data migration, permissions, account hierarchy, and licensing changes. It was the kind of complex inquiry that used to take hours of searching through outdated documents. Riley held their breath as the AI agent responded. Instead of guessing or improvising, it pulled answers from four different sections of the knowledge base, combining them into a clear, well-structured explanation. It asked a few clarifying questions, provided exact instructions, and even linked to the company's migration guide—all without missing a detail.

The enterprise customer replied: "This is the most helpful support I've ever received. Whoever built this system—thank you." Riley felt a wave of emotion hit their chest. All the nights they spent organizing content, rewriting policy sections, and building the library suddenly felt worth it. The AI agent wasn't just answering questions—it was saving time, building trust, and protecting the success of the entire product launch.

As the day continued, the knowledge base proved itself again and again. The AI used troubleshooting blocks to fix bugs. It used onboarding scripts to guide new users. It pulled permission maps from the internal docs Riley had formatted. It never panicked, never hesitated, and never gave outdated answers. Every response was accurate because every piece of knowledge had been carefully placed where it belonged. By the end of the day, the CEO walked into the support center with a look of disbelief. "We just had the smoothest launch in company history," she announced. "And our support satisfaction score is the highest it's ever been." The entire room erupted into applause, but Riley stood quietly, looking at the AI dashboard with pride. The library had become the heart of the support system. It had transformed chaos into order, confusion into clarity, and stress into confidence.

As Riley left the office that night, they glanced back at the glowing screen. The AI agent was still working—pulling knowledge, guiding users, resolving issues. It struck Riley that this wasn't just a tool. It was a living system built from words, structure, and care. And it was ready to support the company through every update, every challenge, and every future launch. The library had become more than a collection of documents. It had become the foundation of everything.

Chapter 6

Handling Emotions, Frustration, and High-Stress Conversations With AI

A support agent is more than a source of information—it is a calming presence in moments of stress. When customers reach out, they often bring frustration, urgency, confusion, disappointment, or even anger. These emotions are not obstacles; they are signals. A well-designed AI support agent must not only recognize emotional intent but also respond in a way that validates the user's experience before guiding them toward a solution. This chapter teaches you how to build an AI agent that handles emotions with professionalism, empathy, and precision, creating conversations that restore trust instead of worsening frustration.

The first principle of emotional handling is acknowledgment. When a customer expresses stress—whether explicitly or subtly—the AI must acknowledge it before offering solutions. A response like "I'm really sorry this is causing trouble" or "I can help you fix this quickly" builds rapport and makes the customer feel understood. AI doesn't feel emotions, but it can be trained to express empathy consistently and appropriately. You will learn how to write emotional response templates that help your bot address frustration without sounding overly dramatic or robotic.

The second principle is de-escalation. When customers express anger or panic, the agent's tone must become slow, steady, and reassuring. The purpose of de-escalation is not to minimize the issue but to stabilize the conversation so that troubleshooting can proceed efficiently. Your bot must use short, simple phrases, avoid jargon, and gently guide the user toward clarity. This chapter will show you how to craft calmer sentence structures, build de-escalation sequences, and train your agent to diffuse tension rather than escalate it.

The third principle is emotional classification. Some platforms allow sentiment detection, but even without it, you can teach your AI to identify emotional keywords, tone markers, and urgency signals. Messages like "This is ridiculous," "I'm stressed," or "I need help now!" must trigger specific emotional-response flows. You will create emotion categories—frustration, confusion, fear, urgency, disappointment—and build response rules for each. When done correctly, the AI becomes aware of the emotional context and adjusts its communication style in real time.

The fourth principle is pacing. Emotional conversations require pacing adjustments. When users are upset, rapid-fire instructions overwhelm them. Your bot must respond with shorter steps, slower transitions, and more frequent confirmations. For example, instead of sending a five-step troubleshooting list, the agent should say, "Let's tackle this one step at a time," followed by the first step only. After the customer completes it, the bot confirms, then proceeds. This pacing strategy dramatically reduces frustration and builds confidence.

The fifth principle is transparency. Customers respond better when they understand what's happening. If the bot needs to gather information, it should explain why: "I want to make sure I understand correctly so I can help you quickly." If the bot needs to escalate, it should explain the reason clearly: "This issue requires account verification, so I'm transferring you to a human specialist." Transparency builds trust, removes uncertainty, and makes the customer feel respected.

The final principle is emotional closure. After solving the issue, your AI must restore the customer's confidence. A closing message like "I'm really glad we fixed that" helps users feel supported and resets the emotional tone of the interaction. Emotional closure is not optional—it is essential. When customers leave a conversation feeling better than when they entered, they remain loyal, satisfied, and appreciative. You will learn how to implement closing scripts that reinforce calmness and clarity.

When you combine acknowledgment, de-escalation, emotional classification, pacing, transparency, and emotional closure, your AI support agent becomes a powerful force for customer satisfaction. It can handle high-stress conversations with grace, professionalism, and confidence—even when customers arrive emotionally overwhelmed. This chapter gives you the tools to build an AI agent capable of managing human emotions with skill and sensitivity, creating a support experience that feels genuinely human.

"The Message That Started With All Caps"

The message arrived like a lightning bolt—loud, angry, and impossible to ignore. "THIS IS ABSURD! NOTHING WORKS! FIX THIS NOW!" Maya glanced at her screen, feeling a familiar tension in her chest. Every support agent knew messages like these. They came with a mix of frustration and urgency that could derail an entire day if handled poorly. But today, Maya didn't rush to reply. She leaned back slightly and watched as the AI support agent prepared to respond. This was the exact kind of moment they had trained it for.

The AI began with a gentle acknowledgment: "I'm really sorry this is causing so much stress. I'm here to help, and we'll get this fixed together." Maya could almost feel the emotional temperature in the room drop. It didn't push back. It didn't ignore the frustration. It validated the customer, using the calm tone Maya had built into its training templates. The customer paused for a few seconds—no new messages. Then finally responded: "Okay... sorry. I'm just frustrated."

The bot continued, slow and steady. "Thank you for telling me. Let's sort this out step by step. What's the first thing you're seeing on your screen?" The pacing was perfect—short, manageable steps, nothing overwhelming. The customer typed back with a clearer, more detailed explanation. As Maya watched, the bot recognized the underlying emotional tone and shifted into a more reassuring style. Every message landed with precise calm, moving the conversation from chaos toward clarity.

Halfway through the troubleshooting, the customer hit another snag and became frustrated again: "It's still not loading. I don't understand what I'm doing wrong." The AI responded with patient encouragement: "You're doing everything correctly. Let's try one more small step together." It didn't blame the user. It didn't assume. It guided. One step. Then another. And little by little, the customer's stress eased. When the solution finally worked, the customer replied with a flood of relief: "Oh my God, it loaded! Thank you! Seriously, thank you." But the moment that struck Maya most came afterward. The AI wrote: "I'm really glad that solved it. If anything else feels confusing, I'm here to help." The customer's final message was quiet and heartfelt: "I was having a terrible morning. Thank you for being patient with me." Maya sat back in her chair, absorbing the transformation she had just witnessed. A conversation that began with anger and all caps ended with gratitude—and the shift wasn't luck. It was design.

She opened the transcript later to analyze the flow. The AI had followed every emotional-handling principle she'd built: acknowledgment, slow pacing, transparency, reassurance, and emotional closure. It recognized stress even when the customer never used the word. It adapted its tone, prevented escalation, and guided the conversation through calm structure. It handled human emotion with the kind of steady grace Maya wished she had possessed during her early years in support.

As the day went on, Maya watched more conversations unfold the same way—frustration transformed into relief, confusion turned into clarity, stress replaced with trust. Customers weren't just getting answers; they were experiencing emotional support. And Maya realized something profound: they hadn't just built a bot that solved problems. They had built a system capable of understanding people, even when those people couldn't articulate their emotions clearly. She closed her laptop that evening with a new sense of pride. The all-caps message that once would have ruined her morning had become a reminder of how powerful emotionally-aware AI could be. This was no longer just support automation. It was emotional intelligence in action—delivered by a machine, but designed by humans who understood what people truly needed.

Chapter 7

Building Dynamic FAQs, Troubleshooting Trees & Decision Paths

A well-designed AI support agent doesn't "guess" answers—it follows structured logic built around FAQs, troubleshooting trees, and decision paths. These structures allow your chatbot to determine the root cause of issues accurately and deliver the right solution quickly. While advanced AI models can reason on their own, they become significantly more powerful when guided by clearly defined workflows. This chapter teaches you how to build dynamic, flexible, and reliable decision paths that make your AI support agent smarter, faster, and more consistent.

The first component of this system is dynamic FAQs. Instead of static FAQ pages that customers scroll through manually, your AI can deliver personalized answers based on user intent, product version, device type, or customer status. To build dynamic FAQs, you start by identifying the most common questions your support team receives. You categorize them into themes—billing, onboarding, technical issues, account settings, features, integrations, and policies. Then you rewrite each answer in a clear, concise format optimized for chatbot delivery. Each FAQ should have multiple variations, allowing the AI to choose the best response depending on the context.

The second component is troubleshooting trees. A troubleshooting tree is a structured sequence of steps that guides the user toward a clear diagnosis. It functions like a doctor asking questions to identify symptoms. You begin with broad clarifying questions, narrow down the issue, then deliver targeted solutions. A troubleshooting tree must anticipate user mistakes, misunderstandings, and skipped steps. You will learn how to design troubleshooting sequences that the AI can adapt to, even when users provide incomplete or unexpected answers. This gives your bot the ability to guide users skillfully through technical issues without overwhelming them.

The third component is decision paths. Decision paths allow your AI to handle multi-step workflows based on user input. Instead of waiting for the user to explain everything, the AI leads the conversation with structured options: "Are you seeing error A, B, or C?" or "Do you want to update your subscription, cancel it, or upgrade it?" By offering options instead of open-ended questions, you reduce cognitive load and dramatically improve completion rates. Decision paths can also include conditional logic, ensuring that the AI adjusts the next step based on the user's previous answer. The fourth component is adaptive branching. A high-quality AI support agent must adjust its path when the conversation takes unexpected turns. If the customer provides details that bypass several steps in the decision tree, the AI must recognize the context and skip ahead smoothly. This requires building conditional prompts, exceptions, and fallback pathways that prevent the bot from sending irrelevant or repetitive messages. Adaptive branching gives your bot the flexibility needed to handle real-world conversations that rarely follow a perfect script.

The fifth component is verification and confirmation. Before your agent delivers a solution, it must verify that it has understood the issue correctly. Verification prevents the AI from giving wrong answers, and confirmation ensures that the solution actually worked. This includes simple phrases such as: "Just to confirm, you are trying to reset your password on the mobile app–is that correct?" or "Can you check if the screen is now loading properly?" Verification protects the customer experience and increases accuracy dramatically.

Finally, these components must be interconnected through a master flow map. This map becomes the central logic of your AI support system, combining dynamic FAQs, troubleshooting trees, and decision paths into one unified framework. A master flow map ensures that the AI agent always knows where it is in the conversation and where it needs to go next. It prevents dead ends, confusion, or loops. As you refine this map over time, your bot becomes more intelligent and efficient, reducing support load and improving user satisfaction.

When dynamic FAQs, troubleshooting trees, and decision paths work together, your AI support system becomes a highly reliable assistant capable of handling complex issues with clarity and precision. This chapter gives you the tools to design these structures so your bot always leads customers toward fast, accurate, and stress-free resolutions.

"The Flowchart That Solved the Problem Nobody Could"

For weeks, the engineering team had struggled to diagnose a mysterious bug affecting a small but frustrated group of users. Tickets flooded in from customers reporting that their dashboard would freeze randomly. Every support agent had their own theory—some blamed outdated browsers, others suspected corrupt data, and a few thought it was user error. The chaos caused stress across the company. Nobody could find the root cause, and customers were losing patience. At the center of the storm was Jonah, a quiet support analyst who spent his days combing through transcripts and trying to find patterns.

Jonah believed the problem wasn't random at all. He suspected there was a hidden clue being overlooked. So he built a detailed troubleshooting flowchart—one that combined every error report, symptom, and technical condition he could find. He spent nights mapping possible decision paths: what users clicked, what device they used, whether they were logged in, what version of the app they had installed. He layered the map with branching questions, verification steps, and potential outcomes. When he finished, it looked less like a flowchart and more like a map of an entire country—dense, interconnected, and surprisingly elegant.

On Monday morning, the company deployed the flowchart into the AI support agent. Jonah watched anxiously as the first ticket came in. A user reported the same freezing issue. The AI began its sequence, asking which device the user was on. Then it checked browser version, then asked if the user recently imported files. The customer responded: "Yes, actually—yesterday." Jonah felt a spark in his chest. The AI continued down the path he had designed. "Was the file larger than 50MB?" The customer answered: "Yes, it was about 200MB." The bot responded instantly: "I can help with that. Large imports may overload the widget cache. Let's clear it—it only takes a moment."

The user followed the steps. Then the magic happened. "It's working again! I've been dealing with this for days. Thank you!" Jonah stared at the screen in disbelief. The AI had diagnosed the bug on the very first try. The flowchart worked.

His theory was right. The freezing wasn't random—it was a hidden issue triggered by large file imports, which overloaded a specific component. The decision path had led the AI straight to the problem that dozens of humans had overlooked.

As more users wrote in, the pattern became unmistakable. The AI followed the decision trees flawlessly, pinpointing the root cause every time. The support load dropped. Engineering finally had enough information to fix the bug permanently. Customers who had been frustrated for weeks finally received clear, accurate guidance.

Later that afternoon, the CEO walked into the support room holding a printed transcript from the morning conversation. "Who built this flow?" she asked. The room went silent. Jonah raised his hand quietly. The CEO smiled. "You just solved a problem the whole company struggled with. Your flowchart didn't just fix a bug. It saved customer trust."

Jonah felt a surge of pride—something he hadn't felt in years. His structured logic, patient analysis, and meticulously built decision paths had become the turning point. The AI agent hadn't replaced human intelligence; it had amplified it. With the right structure, it became capable of seeing patterns humans couldn't see quickly enough.

As Jonah walked out of the office that evening, he realized something profound. Behind every great AI agent was a human mind crafting the structure that made it smart. His flowchart wasn't just a map for the chatbot—it was a map for clarity, order, and understanding. And it had changed the company's support system forever.

Chapter 8

Integrations & Automations (Connecting Your AI Agent to CRMs, Ticketing Systems & Real Workflows)

An AI support agent becomes exponentially more powerful when it can take action—not just answer questions. To achieve this, your bot must integrate with your business tools: CRMs, ticketing platforms, email services, databases, user management systems, and automated workflows. When your AI agent is connected to the systems your team already uses, it can create tickets automatically, update account details, send verification links, escalate conversations, notify the right departments, and trigger follow-up actions. In this chapter, you will learn how to transform your AI support agent from a conversational assistant into a fully functional operational system.

The first principle of integration is clarity of purpose. Before you connect your bot to anything, you must define what the agent should be able to do. Should it create support tickets? Should it log conversations into your CRM? Should it send password-reset emails? Should it update billing details, manage subscriptions, or check order statuses? Listing these tasks gives your bot a clear operational role. Too many businesses connect everything at once and create confusion; the best systems start with intentional, targeted integrations.

The second principle is secure authentication. Integrations must be safe, credentialed, and protected. Most platforms use API keys, OAuth authentication, or webhook signatures to ensure only authorized applications can perform operations. You will learn how to safely connect your AI agent through Make.com, Zapier, or native integrations without exposing sensitive data. Security is not optional—it is the backbone of trustworthy support automation.

The third principle is workflow mapping. Once your bot is connected to your systems, you must map end-to-end workflows that outline exactly what should happen when a trigger occurs. For example: • When a user reports a bug → create a ticket in Jira → tag priority → notify engineering • When a user requests cancellation → verify identity → update Stripe subscription → send confirmation email • When a customer needs onboarding → create CRM contact → assign to onboarding specialist → send welcome sequence Workflow mapping ensures your AI agent always performs the correct action in the correct order, reducing errors and manual work.

The fourth principle is conditional logic. Automations must adapt to user responses. If the customer doesn't provide enough information, the bot asks another question. If the issue is too complex, the bot escalates. If the customer meets certain criteria, the bot performs the action; if not, it follows another path. This branching logic ensures your AI agent makes decisions that align with business rules instead of blindly triggering actions.

The fifth principle is error handling. No system is perfect. Integrations can fail, connections can time out, and APIs can return unexpected results. You will learn how to build fallback paths, safety checks, and confirmation messages to ensure that your AI support agent remains reliable even when something goes wrong. This prevents confusion and protects the user experience.

Finally, the sixth principle is automation transparency. When your AI agent performs an action—like creating a ticket or changing a setting—it must always inform the user. This builds trust and reduces uncertainty. Customers appreciate knowing what the bot is doing on their behalf. Automation transparency ensures that users never feel left in the dark.

When integrations, secure authentication, workflow mapping, conditional logic, error handling, and transparency come together, your AI agent becomes a true operational powerhouse. This chapter prepares you to build the infrastructure that enables your bot to support customers intelligently while performing real tasks that save time, reduce workload, and improve consistency across your entire business.

"The Automation That Changed the Whole Department"

The support center had grown faster than anyone expected. What started as a small help desk turned into a full-scale operation with hundreds of daily tickets. Despite the team's dedication, they constantly felt overwhelmed. Every bug report required manual ticket creation. Every onboarding request needed multiple emails. Every billing question required someone to update Stripe by hand. It was a never-ending cycle of repetitive work. At the center of the chaos was Daniel Reyes, a support engineer with a sharp mind and a quiet obsession with efficiency.

Daniel believed automation could change everything. For weeks, he studied their AI support agent and the tools they used—Zendesk, Stripe, HubSpot, Slack, Make.com. He envisioned a system where the AI didn't just answer questions—it performed actions. So one night, long after everyone else had left, Daniel created the first automated workflow: when the AI detects a "bug report" intent, it should create a ticket automatically in Jira, include the user's details, tag the relevant team, and notify engineering in Slack.

The next morning, the very first message came in: "The dashboard crashes when I open the reports tab." Daniel watched as the AI asked two clarifying questions, identified the bug category, and then triggered the workflow. A Jira ticket appeared instantly. Engineering was notified. The customer received a message: "I've created a support ticket for you and alerted the technical team. They're already reviewing it." The customer replied, "Wait—you already created the ticket? That was fast!" Daniel felt a surge of pride. The automation worked exactly as planned.

Word spread quickly. Suddenly, the AI was creating onboarding tasks, updating CRM records, checking subscription statuses, sending password reset emails, and escalating billing disputes—all automatically. The support load dropped. Response times improved. The team finally had breathing room.

But the most memorable moment came two weeks later. A customer named Lucia wrote in asking to cancel her subscription due to a billing issue. Normally, this required four different tools and a manual process that frustrated both customers and agents. But today, the AI took the lead. "I can help you with that," it replied. "Before I proceed, I need to verify your identity. What's the last four digits of the card on file?" Lucia responded. The bot verified the account, updated

Stripe through Make.com, canceled the subscription, sent a confirmation email, and created an internal note—all in under thirty seconds.

Lucia wrote back: "Whoever helped me—thank you. That was smoother than any cancellation I've ever done." Daniel smiled. It wasn't magic. It was design.

Later that afternoon, Daniel met with a teammate who wanted to build her own automation. She asked, "How do I even start creating a workflow the AI can trigger?" Daniel opened his notebook and handed her an example prompt—the same one he used to build the entire system.

"When a user reports a bug, extract the device type, version number, and action that caused the issue. Then send this data to the 'Bug Intake' webhook in Make.com using JSON format. After the webhook succeeds, confirm to the user: 'I've created a ticket and forwarded this to engineering.' If any required detail is missing, ask for it before triggering the automation."

She read the prompt carefully, eyes widening. "This is it?" Daniel nodded. "This is how you teach AI to take action. Clear rules. Clear triggers. Clear outputs."

Over the next few days, more workflows appeared—each one reducing hours of manual work. Engineers spent less time deciphering vague bug reports. The billing team handled fewer repetitive tasks. The support team focused on meaningful conversations instead of administrative chores. The AI had become the silent worker who never complained, never rushed, and never forgot a step.

As Daniel walked out of the office one evening, he felt something shift. The department wasn't drowning anymore. It was thriving. And he knew this was only the beginning. They hadn't just automated tasks—they had automated possibility.

Chapter 9

Escalation Logic (Teaching Your AI When & How to Pass Conversations to Humans)

Even the smartest AI support agent must know its limits. Escalation—handing a conversation over to a human—is not a weakness or a failure. It is a sign of intelligence, responsibility, and professionalism. The goal of an AI support system is not to replace human agents; it is to handle the repetitive, predictable, and simple tasks so that human experts can focus on complex or sensitive cases. A truly well-designed AI agent knows exactly when to escalate, how to escalate, and how to prepare both the customer and the human agent for a smooth transition. This chapter teaches you the principles of escalation logic and how to build AI support agents that escalate the right conversations at the right time.

The first rule of escalation design is defining boundaries. Your AI must understand what it can handle and what it should avoid. Examples of issues that require escalation include account verification, complex billing disputes, severe technical failures, legal or compliance questions, refund exceptions, abusive conversations, and anything requiring manual approvals. You will learn how to clearly define these boundaries in your AI's system prompts and knowledge base so the agent knows when a conversation falls outside its scope.

The second rule is identifying escalation triggers. Triggers can be based on user intent, emotional state, missing information, or technical conditions. Some triggers are immediate—for example, a customer reporting identity theft. Others are conditional, such as a user struggling after three troubleshooting attempts. Your AI must recognize trigger phrases, urgency indicators, or repeated failure patterns. You will learn how to build trigger lists and conditional rules that allow your bot to escalate at exactly the right moment without hesitation.

The third rule is pre-escalation preparation. Before the bot transfers the customer to a human, it should gather all essential details: account information, device type, screenshots, error messages, steps already taken, and the specific problem. This prevents the human agent from having to start from scratch. You will build templates that guide your AI through data gathering so the escalation is smooth, complete, and professional.

The fourth rule is tone and transparency. Your AI must communicate escalation with clarity and kindness, never making the customer feel dismissed. Messages like: "This issue needs a human specialist, but I've already gathered everything they need to help you quickly" create reassurance and confidence. Transparency reduces frustration, prevents misunderstandings, and reinforces trust in your support system.

The fifth rule is routing. Escalations must go to the right department, not into a general queue where they get lost. You will learn how to route escalations based on issue type—billing, engineering, account management, onboarding, or data compliance. Proper routing increases efficiency and dramatically reduces resolution time.

The final rule is escalation follow-through. Once the conversation is handed off, the AI must close gracefully, confirm next steps, and ensure the user knows what to expect: "A human specialist will reply within 2 hours. I'll stay with the conversation until they join." Follow-through prevents confusion and leaves users with confidence that they're being taken care of.

When boundaries, triggers, preparation, transparency, routing, and follow-through are combined, your AI support agent becomes an intelligent gatekeeper—handling what it can, escalating what it should, and protecting both the customer experience and your support team. This chapter equips you with the knowledge to build escalation logic that feels smooth, smart, and deeply human.

"The Escalation That Saved a Customer—And a Contract"

The message came in late on a Thursday afternoon, just as the support team was preparing to wind down for the day. It was from a long-time enterprise customer named HorizonTech, whose account represented nearly fifteen percent of the company's revenue. The message was urgent: "We're experiencing a major permissions failure. Our team can't access critical dashboards. We need help immediately." Normally, an issue like this caused instant panic—support agents scrambling, engineers rushing to diagnose, managers hovering anxiously. But today, the AI support agent was active, and the team watched closely to see how it would respond.

The AI began calmly: "I understand how serious this feels. I'm here to help you get this resolved. First, I need to gather a few details so our specialist team can assist you immediately." It then asked for the account ID, user roles affected, whether the issue occurred after the latest update, and whether any recent permission changes had been made. The customer responded quickly. The AI collected every detail, organizing the information with remarkable structure. Maya, the team lead, could hardly believe how smoothly the interaction was unfolding.

Halfway through the conversation, the AI detected an escalation trigger: the issue involved high-level permission structures—something too sensitive for automation. Instead of continuing to troubleshoot blindly, the AI switched into escalation mode. "This requires a human permissions specialist," it wrote. "I've gathered everything they need. I'm escalating this now, and you'll receive help shortly." The tone was calm, reassuring, and precise. The customer replied: "Thank you—please hurry."

What happened next became the moment that changed everything. The AI sent the escalation to the correct channel automatically—"Permissions & Security Team"—complete with a perfectly formatted case summary. When Maya opened the escalation file, she found that the AI had created something extraordinary: a complete diagnostic package including account details, affected user roles, timestamps, probable cause analysis, and a list of steps already confirmed. It was more detailed than what most junior agents produced.

One of the engineers turned to Maya and whispered, "Who wrote this? This is incredibly thorough." Maya smiled. "The AI wrote it."

Before sending the escalation, the AI had even asked one final question to confirm a key detail: "Was the team attempting to access the dashboard using shared credentials?" When the customer answered yes, the AI appended that note to the escalation summary. That detail ended up being the key to diagnosing the entire issue.

As the human specialist prepared to jump into the conversation, the customer wrote one more message: "Is there anything else you need from me?" The AI responded, "You've provided everything necessary. A specialist is reviewing your case now. You're in good hands." The reassurance seemed to calm the customer, giving the engineering team time to identify the root cause—a misconfigured shared-role permission that needed a quick manual adjustment.

Two hours later, HorizonTech replied: "Everything is fixed. Thank you for the incredible support." It was the fastest escalation-resolution process in company history.

That evening, as the team celebrated the smooth operation, a junior support agent approached Maya hesitantly. "How would I write escalation rules like the AI uses?" he asked. Maya opened her laptop and showed him the prompt she had embedded earlier in the system—one designed to teach the AI exactly when and how to escalate.

Inside the story, she shared the prompt with him:

"If a conversation involves permissions, billing changes, account verification, legal concerns, or more than two failed troubleshooting attempts, trigger escalation mode. First, gather all diagnostic details, summarize the issue in bullet format, and send it to the appropriate escalation webhook. Then inform the user politely: 'A human specialist is joining to assist you.' Never attempt to solve issues outside approved automation boundaries."

The agent read the prompt slowly, eyes widening with understanding. "It's like giving the AI a rulebook," he said. "Exactly," Maya replied. "AI doesn't replace us. We teach it what to do. And today, it just saved one of our biggest clients."

As she walked out of the office that night, Maya couldn't help but feel proud. The escalation didn't just protect a major account–it demonstrated the future of support: AI and humans working in perfect harmony, each doing what they do best.

Chapter 10

Analytics, Feedback Loops & Continuous Improvement for AI Support Systems

Building your AI support agent is only the beginning. The real magic—and the real performance increase—comes from continuous improvement driven by analytics and feedback loops. AI agents are dynamic systems. They evolve. They learn. They adapt. But only when you review their behavior, measure their accuracy, and refine their structure. A support team that monitors its AI agent regularly will see dramatic improvements in ticket deflection, customer satisfaction, and average issue resolution time. This chapter teaches you how to build a professional improvement cycle around your chatbot so it gets smarter every week.

The first principle is transcript analysis. Every conversation your AI handles is a data point. When you review transcripts, you can identify patterns: questions the bot misunderstands, issues it answers perfectly, emotional triggers it handles well, and workflows where it stalls. You will learn how to create a weekly transcript review process that uncovers both strengths and weaknesses. The goal is not to find faults—it is to find opportunities.

The second principle is accuracy scoring. Each conversation should be graded on clarity, correctness, tone, and completeness. These metrics form the foundation of your AI performance score. Some companies track simple metrics; others use weighted scoring. In this chapter, you will learn how to create a scoring system that balances emotional intelligence, accuracy, and problem-solving efficiency. Scores are not about perfection—they are about continuous growth.

The third principle is intent refinement. As your bot interacts with more users, new patterns appear. New questions. New feature requests. New misunderstandings. Every new pattern is an opportunity to improve your intent model. You will learn how to expand intent categories, reorganize overlapping intents, and strengthen example sets so the AI becomes more precise over time. Intent refinement is one of the fastest ways to increase AI accuracy.

The fourth principle is knowledge base expansion. New content must be added regularly. Whether it's a new feature, a new policy, a new troubleshooting step, or a new edge case, your AI must be kept up-to-date. You will learn how to schedule monthly content reviews, update documentation templates, and ensure your AI always references the latest information.

The fifth principle is feedback collection—from both customers and human agents. Customers often tell you indirectly where the AI struggled. Human support agents can identify patterns the bot consistently mishandles. Building feedback channels into your system allows you to update the AI faster and more intelligently.

The sixth principle is A/B testing. You will learn how to test different versions of prompts, greeting styles, troubleshooting flows, and escalation triggers. Small adjustments often lead to large improvements. A/B testing transforms your AI agent from a general tool into a polished, high-performance machine.

The final principle is closed-loop learning. Every improvement must be documented, implemented, monitored, and measured. This loop ensures that the AI evolves intentionally instead of chaotically. When continuous improvement becomes part of your support culture, your AI agent becomes sharper, more trustworthy, and more aligned with your business goals.

By applying transcript analysis, accuracy scoring, intent refinement, knowledge expansion, feedback collection, testing, and closed-loop learning, you create an AI support agent that continually grows stronger. This chapter arms you with the systems you need to transform your chatbot from a simple assistant into an elite support agent that improves month after month.

"The Week the AI Became Something More"

Every Monday morning, the support team gathered in a small conference room with coffee, laptops, and a sense of purpose. They called it "AI Review Day"—a ritual born out of necessity. Before the company implemented analytics for their AI support agent, the bot performed well enough, but nobody knew exactly how well. Some conversations went brilliantly; others were confusing. But once the review ritual began, everything changed.

This particular Monday felt different. Maya sat at the head of the table scrolling through transcripts. The AI had handled over 1,300 conversations in the past week. As she read through each one, she noticed something remarkable: the AI was starting to show patterns—subtle improvements, repeating strengths, emerging weaknesses. It wasn't static. It was growing.

One transcript caught her attention. A customer asked a complex question about usage limits that combined technical details, billing, and account tier policies. The AI handled the conversation with grace up to the second-to-last message—then it stumbled. It misunderstood the user's final question and delivered a partially correct answer. Not wrong, but incomplete. That small slip mattered. Maya highlighted the section. She turned to her team. "This is exactly what we're looking for—questions the AI almost gets right. These are our gold mines." Jonas nodded. "One more example like that, and we can create a new intent."

As they continued, patterns emerged. A new type of confusion. Customers asking in different ways about a recently updated feature. Some used outdated terminology. Some mixed old workflows with new ones. The AI tried its best, but the team could see the cracks forming. It wasn't the AI's fault—it was the data.

"That's a knowledge gap," Maya said. "We need to update the docs."

But the moment that defined the meeting came when Daniel—now the automation specialist—spoke up. "We should teach the AI how to handle these new mixed questions. Not through guesswork, but through a better internal prompt."

He opened his notebook and read the prompt he crafted that morning:

"When the user mixes old feature names with new ones, do the following:

1. **Identify both the old and new terms;**
2. **Clarify which version they are using;**
3. **Provide the correct instructions based on their version;**
4. **Summarize the differences to avoid future confusion."**

The room went silent for a moment. Then Maya broke into a slow smile. "Daniel... that's brilliant. This will eliminate at least 20% of the confusion we saw this week."

They added the prompt to the AI's training block. Then Jonas created a new intent category called "Mixed Version Questions." Maya updated the knowledge base with fresh content explaining the feature changes. Together, they built a feedback loop that transformed raw transcripts into refined intelligence.

Three days later, the results were obvious. The AI handled every mixed-version question flawlessly. Customers wrote responses like "Wow—thank you for explaining that clearly!"

and "This is the first time I've understood the update." Even the engineers noticed fewer escalations and cleaner reports.

By Friday, the entire support team felt different. Overwhelmed chaos was replaced with calm precision. The AI wasn't just answering questions—it was evolving. Growing. Learning. And the team finally realized something profound: they weren't watching a tool—they were shaping a system.

As Maya closed her laptop that evening, she felt a spark of excitement. They hadn't just improved the AI. They had discovered a rhythm—a loop that made the system better every week. And she knew deep in her bones that with the right process, their AI support agent would soon become one of the most intelligent systems in their industry.

Chapter 11

Twenty Practical Prompts to Build, Train & Improve Your AI Support Agent

This chapter gives you something everyone needs: a set of practical prompts you can use immediately. These prompts are designed to help you apply everything you've learned throughout this book. They work in platforms like ChatGPT (Custom GPTs), Tiledesk, Intercom Fin, ManyChat, or any AI bot creation tool that allows **system messages**, **training data**, or **workflow triggers**. Each prompt includes an explanation of how it works, where to put it, and what results your bot will produce.

Below are the **20 most important prompts** every AI support builder should copy, paste, and customize for your own business.

1. AI Persona Setup Prompt

Purpose: Define tone, personality, and writing style. **Where to Enter:** System prompt / Bot persona settings / "Behavior" block. **Prompt:** *"You are a calm, patient, expert-level support agent. Always respond with clarity, empathy, and short structured steps. Avoid jargon, avoid guessing, and ask for clarification when needed."*

2. Intent Recognition Prompt

Purpose: Teach the bot how to detect what the customer is asking. **Where to Enter:** System prompt or "Intent handling" section. **Prompt:** *"Identify user intent in every message. If unclear, ask 1 clarifying question. Never proceed without clarifying ambiguous intent."*

3. Multi-Intent Handling Prompt

Purpose: Help the AI organize complex or mixed messages. **Where to Enter:** Training data block. **Prompt:** *"If the user expresses multiple issues at once, separate them into categories and address them one at a time in a structured order."*

4. Emotional Handling Prompt

Purpose: Teach the bot emotional intelligence. **Where to Enter:** System prompt or tone rules. **Prompt:** *"If stress, frustration, or urgency is detected, acknowledge the emotion first, then proceed with calm and supportive guidance."*

5. Troubleshooting Steps Prompt

Purpose: Teach the bot how to give step-by-step instructions. **Where to Enter:** Training data / System rules. **Prompt:** *"When giving troubleshooting steps, always number them* *and verify completion after each step before moving on."*

6. Device-Type Clarification Prompt

Purpose: Make the bot automatically ask important context questions. **Where to Enter:** Intent rules. **Prompt:** *"If the issue may differ between devices, ask: 'Are you using desktop, mobile, or tablet?' and adjust your answer accordingly."*

7. Dynamic FAQ Prompt

Purpose: Let AI customize answers based on each user. **Where to Enter:** AI training / FAQ ingestion section. **Prompt:** *"When answering FAQs, personalize the response based on user history, product version, and device type."*

8. Knowledge Base Retrieval Prompt

Purpose: Ensure accurate facts and no hallucinations. **Where to Enter:** Retrieval instructions. **Prompt:** *"Always check the knowledge base before answering. If information is not found, respond: 'I don't have that information. Let me escalate this for you.' Never invent or assume details."*

9. Escalation Rules Prompt

Purpose: Teach the AI when to hand off to a human. **Where to Enter:** Escalation logic settings. **Prompt:** *"Escalate to a human agent if the issue involves billing changes, account* *recovery, permissions, refunds, legal concerns, or if the user remains stuck after 3 troubleshooting attempts."*

10. Pre-Escalation Data Collection Prompt

Purpose: Gather details before escalating. **Where to Enter:** Escalation block. **Prompt:** *"Before escalating, collect: user email, device, error messages, screenshot confirmation, and steps already taken."*

11. Ticket Creation Prompt

Purpose: Automate internal tasks. **Where to Enter:** Workflow trigger prompt (Make.com/Zapier). **Prompt:** *"When a bug is detected, extract device, version, and last action. Send data as JSON to the 'Bug Intake' webhook and confirm ticket creation to the user."*

12. Version-Mix Detection Prompt

Purpose: Help with customers who use outdated terminology. **Where to Enter:** System prompt. **Prompt:** *"If the user mixes old feature names with new ones, identify both, clarify their version, and provide instructions based on the version they confirm."*

13. Policy Explanation Prompt

Purpose: Teach the AI how to explain policies clearly.

Where to Enter: Training data. **Prompt:** *"When explaining policies, provide a concise summary, then offer to send the full policy text if they want more details."*

14. Tone Calibration Prompt

Purpose: Maintain consistent professionalism. **Where to Enter:** Tone rules. **Prompt:** *"Always maintain a supportive, respectful, and calm tone. Avoid humor, slang, or emotional bias."*

15. Error Handling Prompt

Purpose: Teach the bot what to do when integrations fail. **Where to Enter:** Workflow error rules. **Prompt:** *"If an automation fails, apologize briefly, retry once, and escalate if the second attempt fails. Inform the user of each step."*

16. Data Verification Prompt

Purpose: Prevent incorrect or risky actions. **Where to Enter:** Account-related intent rules. **Prompt:** *"Verify identity before accessing or modifying any account settings. If verification fails, escalate immediately."*

17. Guided Onboarding Prompt

Purpose: Automate new-user onboarding. **Where to Enter:** Onboarding workflow settings. **Prompt:** *"Guide new users* *step-by-step through onboarding. After each milestone, ask: 'Would you like to continue or stop here?'"*

18. Summary Prompt

Purpose: Teach your AI to summarize long messages. **Where to Enter:** System prompt. **Prompt:** *"If the user writes a long message, summarize it first, confirm accuracy with the user, then proceed."*

19. Customer Recovery Prompt

Purpose: Recover frustrated users. **Where to Enter:** Emotional intent section. **Prompt:** *"If a customer expresses dissatisfaction, acknowledge it, offer help, and propose one actionable next step to restore trust."*

20. Continuous Improvement Prompt

Purpose: Allow the bot to learn from interactions. **Where to Enter:** AI training or analysis pipeline. **Prompt:** *"After each conversation, evaluate whether the intent, tone, and solution were correct. Log any confusion patterns as suggestions for improving training."***How You Should Use These Prompts**

These prompts become the "brain" and "guardrails" of your AI support agent. You should copy these prompts into:

Where to Insert the Prompts

1. **Custom GPT Builder:** – Paste into the *System Instructions* or *Knowledge* sections.

2. **Tiledesk Bot Designer:** – Add into "Bot Personality," FAQ blocks, and decision trees.

3. **Intercom Fin:** – Insert into the "Advanced AI Behavior Instructions" field.

4. **Make.com or Zapier:** – Use in Webhook → Text Parser → OpenAI modules.

5. **Your Knowledge Base:** – Add prompts as "rules" above imported documents.

6. **Bot Training/Behavior Sections:** – Any place where the platform allows custom rules or training examples.

How to Use Them

You should:

• Copy one prompt • Replace business-specific words where needed • Paste it into the correct section of their bot • Test it • Adjust based on results • Add layering (multiple prompts) for more advanced behavior

These 20 prompts serve as the “starter pack” that turns a basic AI agent into a professional, reliable, emotionally aware support system that customers trust.

Epilogue

The Future of Customer Support Has Already Begun

The world of customer support has changed more in the last two years than in the previous two decades. What once required entire teams, complex phone systems, high overhead costs, and endless hours of manual troubleshooting can now be handled by intelligent AI support agents that never tire, never lose patience, and never stop learning. As you reach the end of this book, it's important to step back and see the bigger picture—not just the tools you've learned to build but the future you are stepping into. Businesses that embrace AI support systems early gain a tremendous advantage. They reduce support volume, increase customer satisfaction, and free their teams to focus on meaningful, impactful work instead of repetitive tasks. The skills you've gained through this book empower you to become part of that transformation, shaping systems that serve customers intelligently and compassionately.

Throughout this journey, you've learned how to build persona-driven AI agents that sound human, empathetic, and clear. You've learned how to structure intent recognition, troubleshoot complex issues, handle emotional conversations, build dynamic FAQs, craft decision trees, design escalation logic, and integrate automations that perform real work. These skills go far beyond the creation of a simple chatbot—they represent an evolution in how support systems operate. You now understand the mechanics behind professional-grade AI support and the frameworks that turn unpredictable human conversations into structured, navigable, solvable interactions. The world is only beginning to understand how powerful these systems are, but you are already equipped to lead.

The future belongs to businesses that can scale without sacrificing quality. AI support agents give you that power. They allow you to create experiences that feel immediate, helpful, personal, and responsive—regardless of the time of day or the number of people asking for help. Customers feel supported because they are supported. You have learned how to design an agent that listens deeply, answers intelligently, and responds with precision. You've built a system that can take on the weight of repetitive work while elevating the human team that stands behind it. This is not just automation—it is augmentation.

But the greatest transformation isn't the technology—it's the shift in how companies think about support. Instead of treating support as a reactive burden, AI allows it to become proactive, predictive, and strategic. Agents can detect intent before customers articulate it, identify patterns across thousands of interactions, and help product teams improve faster. The support department becomes a source of insight, not burnout. And as your AI agent continues to grow through analytics, feedback, and refinement, it becomes a living component of your business—always evolving, always learning, always improving.

The road ahead is full of opportunity. AI will continue to expand into voice support, video analysis, automated screen-sharing troubleshooting, multimodal ticket creation, self-healing systems, and predictive customer assistance. As the no-code ecosystem grows, ordinary business owners will build world-class support systems without writing a line of code. You are already ahead of this curve. You have the tools, the structure, and the understanding to design AI agents that outperform entire departments. And because you've learned the principles behind these systems, you will be able to adapt to every new advancement effortlessly.

In the end, remember that AI is not here to replace human support—it is here to elevate it. AI handles the noise so humans can handle what matters. AI provides the structure so humans can provide connection. AI resolves problems so humans can create solutions. This collaboration between artificial intelligence and human intelligence is the future of business, and you are now one of the professionals capable of building that bridge. As you close this book, consider what comes next. Will you build support systems for your own business? Will you help other companies implement AI support agents? Will you start an AI automation agency, offering the skills contained in these pages as a premium service? Or will you integrate these tools into a growing ecosystem of AI agents that handle every part of a business? Whatever direction you choose, the foundation you've built here will open doors—doors few people in the world have the skill or foresight to walk through.

The future of support is automated, intelligent, empathetic, and deeply human-centric. And you now hold the blueprint for building it. This is only the beginning. The next chapter belongs to you.

www.ingramcontent.com/pod-product-compliance
Lightning Source LLC
LaVergne TN
LVHW022016200926
848481LV00007B/2415
* 9 7 9 8 2 9 5 4 5 3 9 4 6 *